discovering  nature

Rivers, Ponds, and Seashore

Sally Hewitt

Copper Beech Books
Brookfield, Connecticut

© Aladdin Books Ltd 1999

Designed and produced by
Aladdin Books Ltd
28 Percy Street
London W1P OLD

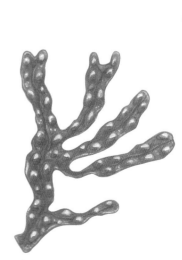

First published in the United States
in 1999 by
Copper Beech Books,
an imprint of
The Millbrook Press
2 Old New Milford Road
Brookfield, Connecticut 06804

Editor: Jon Richards

Consultant: Helen Taylor

Design: David West
CHILDREN'S BOOK DESIGN

Designer: Simon Morse

Photography: Roger Vlitos

Illustrators: Tony Kenyon, Stuart Squires – SGA
& Mike Atkinson

Printed in Belgium

**Cataloging-in-Publication Data is on
file at the Library of Congress**

ISBN 0-7613-0924-1 (lib.bdg.)

5 4 3 2 1

Contents

Introduction

Rivers, ponds, and the sea are full of all kinds of life. You can have fun learning about the things that live and grow on, by, or under the water. Go pond dipping and look out for insects skating on the water. Spot waterbirds, build a dam, and find out about the moon and the tides.

1 Look out for numbers like this. They will guide you through the step-by-step instructions for the projects and activities, making sure that you do things in the right order.

Further facts

Whenever you see this "nature spotters" sign, you will find interesting facts and information to help you understand more about rivers, ponds, and the seashore, and the creatures that live there.

Hints and tips

•Never visit rivers, ponds, or the seashore without an adult. Keep away from steep, slippery river banks. Always be careful of deep, fast-flowing water and changing tides.

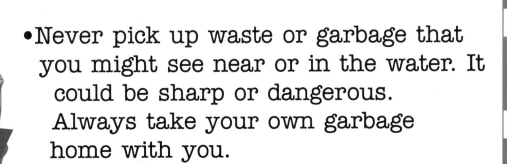

•Never pick up waste or garbage that you might see near or in the water. It could be sharp or dangerous. Always take your own garbage home with you.

•Be patient and still when you are spotting animals. Movement and noises will scare them away.

BE AWARE OF FAST OR STRONG TIDES

Wherever you see this sign, ask an adult to help you. Never use sharp tools or go exploring by yourself.

Get an adult to help you

This special warning sign indicates where you have to take extra care when doing the project. For example, you should always be careful around the seashore – fast and powerful tides could cut you off from land or sweep you out to sea!

Flowing water

When water from rain, melted snow, lakes, and springs collects together, it becomes a river, carving its way through the earth as it flows downhill. See how a river can change the landscape with this project.

Make a river

1 Watch water flowing downhill. Pile up some stones of different sizes at one end of a plastic tray to make a hill.

2 Cover the stones with soil. Shape the soil so that you have a hill sloping down to the opposite edge of the tray.

3 Put some stones down the side of the hill on top of the soil. Now fill a jug with water and pour it on the top of the hill.

4 Watch as the water becomes a mini-river, making channels, and carrying soil downhill.

Fresh and salty water

Rainwater and the water in rivers, lakes, and springs is the water we drink and that plants need to grow. It is called freshwater, which means it is not salty.

Rivers wash salts and minerals from the land into the sea, making it salty. Saltwater is not good to drink!

Dams

When a dam is built across a river, it slows down the flow of water. Water builds up behind the dam to make a lake. We are not the only ones to build dams – some animals find blocking a river very useful!

Dam that river

1 Make a dam by blocking the river on the hill you made on pages 6-7 with a piece of wood.

2 Pour water down the hill and watch it make a little pond behind the dam.

Eager beaver!

A beaver's body is very good for a life in the water. It has webbed feet to swim with, thick waterproof fur, and a flat tail, like a paddle, which it uses to steer when it's in the water.

Beavers are clever builders. They cut down trees with their strong, sharp teeth and drag them into the river to make a dam.

Beavers build dams to make lakes, which surround their homes and make them safe from enemies.

A beaver's home, called a lodge, is a mound of sticks and mud in the middle of a lake. Underwater tunnels lead up to a dry room inside.

Speedy rivers

Rivers are always on the move. Sometimes they drift slowly along, but at other times they can turn into a rushing torrent. This project will help you to measure the speeds of a river.

Timing sticks

1 Tie different colored string or ribbon tightly onto the end of some short sticks. Take them to a bridge over a river or stream.

DON'T STAND TOO CLOSE TO THE EDGE OF A RIVER!

2 With a friend, try to drop the sticks in the middle and at both sides of the water all at the same time.

3 Time how long it takes for the sticks to appear on the other side of the bridge. Which is the quickest?

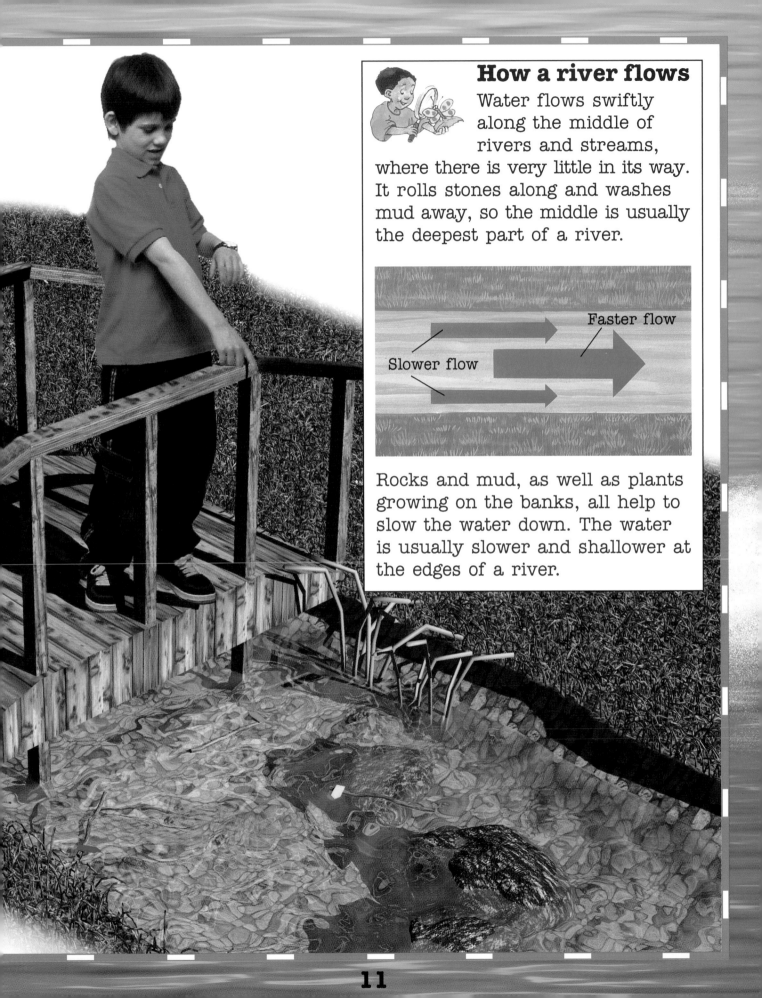

How a river flows

Water flows swiftly along the middle of rivers and streams, where there is very little in its way. It rolls stones along and washes mud away, so the middle is usually the deepest part of a river.

Faster flow

Slower flow

Rocks and mud, as well as plants growing on the banks, all help to slow the water down. The water is usually slower and shallower at the edges of a river.

Pond dipping

Spring or summer are the best times to go pond dipping. With just a net and a plastic container, you will find all kinds of plants and animals living in every part of the pond.

DON'T LEAN TOO FAR OVER THE WATER – YOU MIGHT FALL IN!

Dippers

1 Fill a clean plastic container with pond water. Sweep your net in the water near the edge of the pond.

2 Empty the net into the container. With a magnifying glass, examine all the plants and creatures you have caught.

3 Now sweep your net nearer the middle of the pond. Have you caught different things?

Pond creatures

Here are just some of the amazing creatures that you might find living in a pond.

Sticklebacks have sharp, spiny fins along their backs.

Great pond snails have rough tongues for eating underwater plants.

Leeches hunt for fishes and snails to feed off.

A **water boatman** swims upside down on the surface of the water.

Mosquito larvae hang just below the water breathing air through a tube.

 **4** Make sure you return all the living things back to the pond. Try to put them back where you found them.

Water bugs

Creatures live in every part of a pond. They live in the mud, swim in the water, and skate over the surface. Flying insects dart above the water and lay their eggs on the water plants.

Spot the creepy crawlies

1 A water spider spins its web underwater and fills it with bubbles of air. Then it lies in wait for a passing creature to catch and eat.

Dragonfly

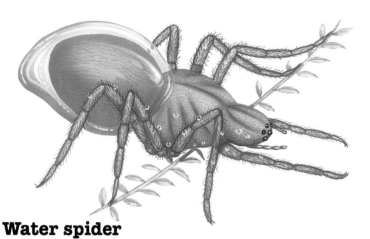

Water spider

2 A dragonfly darts above the water catching insects with its legs. It has see-through wings and a shiny, colorful body.

3 A whirligig beetle whirls around on the water as it hunts for food.

Whirligig

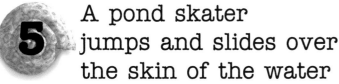

Gnat

4 Female gnats suck a tiny amount of blood for a meal from animals or people. They lay their eggs on the water.

5 A pond skater jumps and slides over the skin of the water without breaking it.

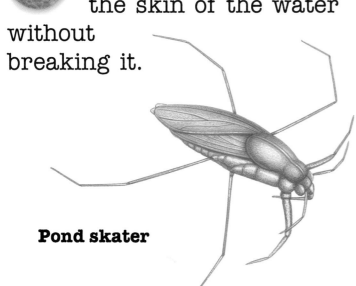

Pond skater

Water skin

Fill a glass to the brim with water so that it is almost overflowing. You can see that the water bulges over the top of the glass as if it has a thin skin.

Pollution in the water breaks up this skin. As a result, creatures like pond skaters that live on the surface cannot live in polluted ponds.

Breathing underwater

Water creatures need to breathe oxygen to live. Some come up to the surface for air, but others stay underwater and breathe the oxygen that is mixed into the water. This project shows you how water plants give off oxygen into the water.

Weedy air

1 You will need pondweed, a funnel, a plastic bottle of water, three lumps of modeling clay, and a see-through container.

2 Put the weed and clay in the bottom of the container and fill with water. Place the funnel on the lumps of clay so that it sits over the pondweed.

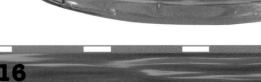

3 Carefully place the bottle of water upside-down over the funnel. Watch how bubbles of oxygen gradually come from the weed and fill the bottle.

Breathing underwater

Fish do not have lungs; they breathe through special organs called gills. These lie just behind the eyes of a fish.

Water flows into the fish's mouth and passes over the gills. Oxygen in the water is taken into the fish's blood as it flows over its gills.

Lungfish have lungs and gills so that they can breathe both in and out of water. If the water they live in dries up, they can hide in the mud until it rains again.

Make a pond

You have already seen some of the plants and animals that live in ponds. Now build one yourself and see if you can attract some of this wildlife to your own pond.

1 You will need a flat tray, gravel, soil, large stones, and some water plants, such as pondweed.

2 Cover the bottom of the tray with gravel and some soil. Use a big stone to make an island in the middle.

3 Carefully fill the tray with water. Try to use rainwater, as it is best for a pond.

4 Add the plants, fixing them with stones and soil. Or you can plant them in the water in little pots.

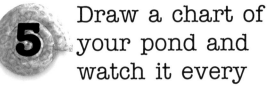

5 Draw a chart of your pond and watch it every day. Keep a note of what animals visit your pond and where they stay, and compare it from day to day.

Frogs

Frogs spend the first part of their lives as tadpoles living underwater. Grown-up frogs live in water and on land.

Frogs lay eggs called frog spawn in the water.

Tadpoles hatch from the eggs and swim underwater.

Tadpoles lose their tails, grow legs, and become little frogs.

19

Waterbirds

Waterbirds live on rivers, ponds, and the seashore. Watch some waterbirds carefully. In what ways are they like this duck? How are they different?

BE CAREFUL NOT TO SCARE ANY WATER BIRDS!

1 This duck has a flat bill. It uses its bill to filter out seeds, insects, and snails from the water to eat.

2 It also uses its bill to spread oil through its feathers to make them waterproof. Drops of water roll easily off the oil.

3 Skin stretched between its three toes turn a duck's feet into a kind of paddle. Many waterbirds have webbed feet like these.

Shapes and sizes

Here are some examples of the different types of waterbirds.

Pelican

A pelican uses its long, strong bill with a pouch like a fishing net to scoop fish out of the water.

Kingfisher

A kingfisher sits on a branch and spots fish to catch in its pointed beak in the water below.

Black-headed gull

A black-headed gull has a hooked bill for catching slippery fish and tearing at food.

Spoonbill

A spoonbill has long, thin legs. It uses these to wade through shallow water, while it picks up food from the bottom with its spoon-shaped bill.

The tide

Driftwood

When you go to the beach, you may notice that the edge of the sea moves backward and forward each day. This is called the tide.

BE AWARE OF FAST OR STRONG TIDES

Shells

Beachcombing

1 When the sea is at low tide, you will see a mark on the sand where the high tide was. Measure the distance between the low tide and the high tide by pacing it out.

Seaweed

Pottery

Pebbles

2 Look at the part of the beach you can only see when the tide is low. You should see small piles of sand made by worms as well as bird tracks.

3 As the sea pulls away from the shore, it leaves all kinds of things behind, such as seaweed and bits of pottery. Make a note of some of the things you find by the sea at low tide.

High and low tide

The tides are actually caused by the sun and the moon.

Gravity is the force that keeps your feet on the ground and causes things to fall to the ground.

The gravity of the sun and the moon pulls the water in the sea, causing tides.

Seaweed

Seaweeds can be found all along the seashore. They do not have roots like plants that grow on land but have special roots, called holdfasts, that grip onto rocks. This project shows you a good way to study seaweed in close-up.

Floating seaweed

1 Collect some seaweed to take home. Find a see-through vase or bottle. Put in the seaweed and use a stone to hold it on the bottom. Now add water.

2 Look at the shape of seaweed when it is held up by water. See how it goes limp and loses its shape out of water.

Types of seaweed

There are three types of seaweed that you can find washed up on the seashore – red, brown, and green.

Carrageen is a red seaweed. You might find some growing in a rock pool.

Bladder wrack is a brown seaweed. It has little pockets of air to help it float upright in the water.

Sea lettuce is a green seaweed that looks like the lettuce leaves we eat.

Rock pools

As the tide goes out it leaves behind pools of water among the rocks. Rock pools are places where you can find creatures and plants hiding. Make your own special viewer to see this underwater world clearly.

TAKE CARE ON THE SLIPPERY ROCKS AROUND ROCK POOLS!

Underwater viewer

1 Cut the top and bottom off a plastic bottle and tape over the rough edges to make your underwater viewer.

Get an adult to help you

2 Pull plastic wrap tightly over one end. Put a rubber band around the plastic wrap to stop it from slipping off your viewer.

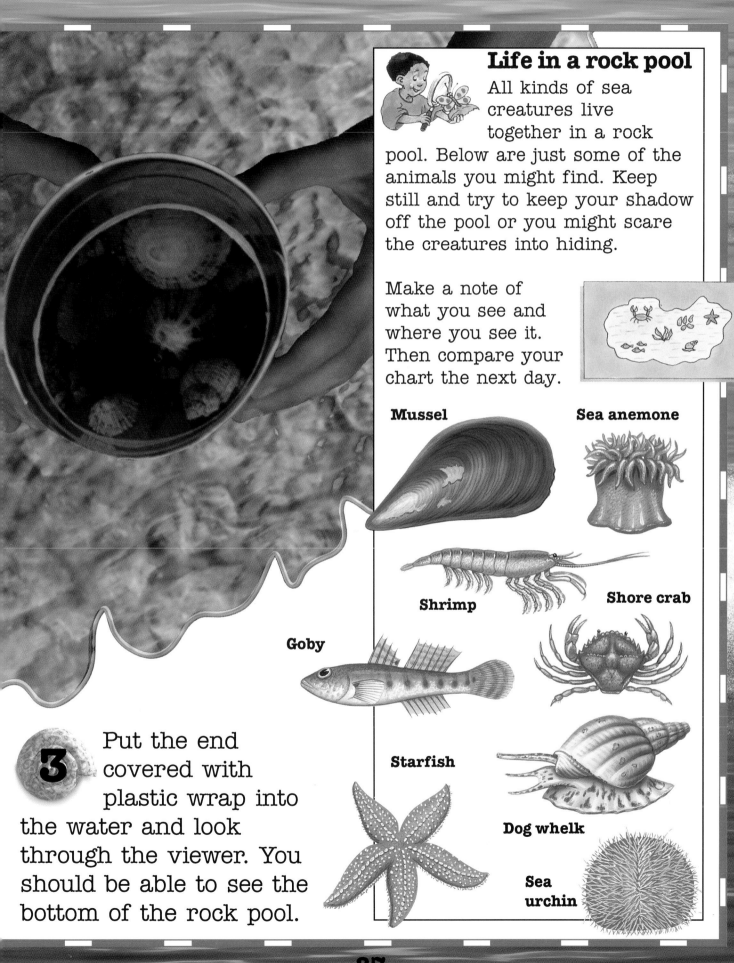

Life in a rock pool

All kinds of sea creatures live together in a rock pool. Below are just some of the animals you might find. Keep still and try to keep your shadow off the pool or you might scare the creatures into hiding.

Make a note of what you see and where you see it. Then compare your chart the next day.

Mussel

Sea anemone

Shrimp

Shore crab

Goby

Starfish

Dog whelk

Sea urchin

3 Put the end covered with plastic wrap into the water and look through the viewer. You should be able to see the bottom of the rock pool.

Shellfish

Shellfish have soft bodies, so they grow a tough shell to protect them. There are many different types of shellfish. Make a collection of shells you find on the beach and sort them into groups like these.

DON'T TAKE SHELLS WITH LIVE CREATURES INSIDE!

Mussels

Scallops

Razor clams

Limpets

4 Scallops, mussels, and razor clams live in shells with hinges. These open up to let the creature feed.

3 Limpets have a single shell to hide under while they cling tightly to a rock.

Collecting shells

1 Arrange your shells into groups depending on each shell's size and shape.

2 These spiral-shaped shells used to be the homes of snail-like animals such as whelks.

Spiral shells

Useful shells

Shellfish have developed some amazing features to feed or protect themselves from creatures who want to eat them.

A **barnacle** waves its legs through a small hole in the top of its shell. It uses these to catch any food which may be floating past.

A **limpet** moves slowly over a rock, scraping off food with its teeth-filled mouth.

A **scallop** escapes from a hungry starfish by flapping its shells open and shut and jet-propelling itself along.

Glossary

Bill

The jaws of a bird are called the bill. There are different types because a bird's bill is specially shaped for the kind of food it eats.

You can see some types of bills by turning to pages 20-21. See if you can spot any other types of bill when you are outside.

Dam

A dam is used to block rivers and streams. Dams can be made from sticks or concrete. Water builds up behind the dam and makes a lake or a pond.

Pages 8-9 show you how to build your own model dam and also which animals build dams to protect their homes.

Freshwater

Freshwater is the water we drink. Rainwater is fresh and so is most of the water found in streams, rivers, ponds, and lakes. Seawater tastes salty because it contains minerals and salts that have been washed off the land and into the sea.

The project on pages 6-7 shows you how rivers wash soil away and carry it down toward the sea, making the water there salty.

Gravity

Gravity is an invisible force that attracts objects to each other. The larger the object, the more gravity it has. The earth's gravity pulls everything down toward the ground.

See how gravity affects the sea on pages 22-23. Can you find out what affects the sea from beyond the earth?

Oxygen

This is an invisible gas found in the air. It is very important because it helps all living things make the energy they need to live.

Turn to pages 16-17 and you can see how water plants give off oxygen. This oxygen dissolves in water and lets fish and other water creatures breathe without having to come to the surface.

Shellfish

These are animals that have soft bodies and need a shell to support their bodies and to protect themselves. Shellfish include crabs, snails, limpets, and scallops.

See how many shells you can collect on your next trip to the beach. Pages 28-29 tell you some amazing facts about sea-living shellfish.

Waterbirds

Birds that swim or wade are called waterbirds. Many, such as ducks, build nests and rear their young on ponds and riverbanks. Seabirds, such as puffins, nest on cliffs along the seashore. Some gulls and waders make nests in small hollows in the sand.

Learn more about waterbirds on pages 20-21.

Tides

The sea moves backward and forward each day. These movements are called the tides.

Have fun examining the seashore between the tides on pages 22-23, and explore the rock pools they leave behind on pages 26-27.

Index